Sports
& Fitness

An Integrated Life of Fitness

Core Workouts

Cross-Training

Eating Right & Additional Supplements for Fitness

Endurance & Cardio Training

Exercise for Physical & Mental Health

Flexibility & Agility

Sports & Fitness

Step Aerobics & Aerobic Dance

Weightlifting & Strength Building

Yoga & Pilates

An Integrated Life of Fitness

Sports & Fitness

CELICIA SCOTT

Mason Crest

Mason Crest
450 Parkway Drive, Suite D
Broomall, PA 19008
www.masoncrest.com

Printed and bound in the United States of America.

9 8 7 6 5 4 3 2

Series ISBN: 978-1-4222-3156-2
Hardcover ISBN: 978-1-4222-3163-0
Paperback ISBN: 978-1-4222-3201-9
ebook ISBN: 978-1-4222-8701-9

Cataloging-in-Publication Data on file with the Library of Congress.

CONTENTS

KEY ICONS TO LOOK FOR:

 Text-Dependent Questions: These questions send the reader back to the text for more careful attention to the evidence presented there.

 Words to Understand: These words with their easy-to-understand definitions will increase the reader's understanding of the text, while building vocabulary skills.

 Series Glossary of Key Terms: This back-of-the book glossary contains terminology used throughout this series. Words found here increase the reader's ability to read and comprehend higher-level books and articles in this field.

 Research Projects: Readers are pointed toward areas of further inquiry connected to each chapter. Suggestions are provided for projects that encourage deeper research and analysis.

 Sidebars: This boxed material within the main text allows readers to build knowledge, gain insights, explore possibilities, and broaden their perspectives by weaving together additional information to provide realistic and holistic perspectives.

INTRODUCTION

Choosing fitness as a priority in your life is one of the smartest decisions you can make! This series of books will give you the tools you need to understand how your decisions about eating, sleeping, and physical activity can affect your health now and in the future.

And speaking of the future: YOU are the future of our world. We who are older are depending on you to build something wonderful—and we, as lifelong advocates of good nutrition and physical activity, want the best for you throughout your whole life.

Our hope in these books is to support and guide you to instill healthy behaviors beginning today. You are in a unique position to adopt healthy habits that will guide you toward better health right now and avoid health-related problems as an adult.

You have the power of choice today. We recognize that it's a very busy world filled with overwhelming choices that sometimes get in the way of you making wise decisions when choosing food or in being active. But no previous training or skills are needed to put this material into practice right away.

We want you to have fun and build your confidence as you read these books. Your self-esteem will increase. LEARN, EXPLORE, and DIS-COVER, using the books as your very own personal guide. A tremendous amount of research over the past thirty years has proven that the quality of your health and life will depend on the decisions you make today that affect your body, mind, and inner self.

You are an individual, liking different foods, doing different things, having different interests, and growing up in different families. But you are not alone as you face these vital decisions in your life. Those of us in the fitness professions are working hard to get healthier foods into your schools; to make sure you have an opportunity to be physically active on a regular basis; to ensure that walking and biking are encouraged in your communities; and to build communities where healthy, affordable foods can be purchased close to home. We're doing all we can to support you. We've got your back!

Moving step by step to healthier eating habits and increasing physical activity requires change. Change happens in small steps, so be patient with yourself. Change takes time. But get started *now*.

Lead an "action-packed" life! Your whole body will thank you by becoming stronger and healthier. You can look and do your best. You'll feel good. You'll have more energy. You'll reap the benefits of smart lifestyle choices for a healthier future so you can achieve what's important to you.

Choose to become the best you can be!

—Diana H. Hart, President
National Association for Health and Fitness

Words to Understand

potential: The possibility of becoming something better.
nutrients: The substances in food that our bodies need to grow and be healthy.

Chapter One
STAYING ACTIVE, STAYING HEALTHY

The human body is a living organism with a lot of **potential**, but it won't become healthy and strong without proper attention. Taking good care of your body has a lot of benefits. Feeling healthier and being able to do more without becoming tired is only the beginning. People with healthy bodies are less likely to get sick, and they usually live a lot longer than people who ignore their bodies' health.

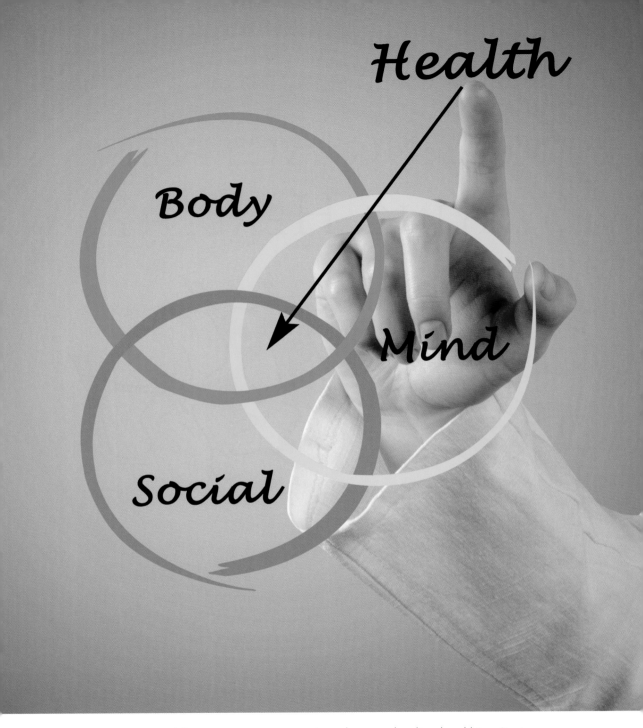

Exercise is good for us in many ways. It makes our bodies healthier. It gives us a chance to make social connections with other people. And it helps us think more clearly.

Make Connections

An important part of keeping the body healthy is giving it time to rest. A human being that doesn't receive enough sleep will feel fatigued and unable to work as hard the next day. The body does most of its rest and recovery during sleep, including fighting off potential illnesses. It is for this reason that the strength of the body's immune system is dependent on getting enough sleep.

Playing sports regularly has also been shown to improve the quality of sleep, and getting enough sleep is an important step to keeping the body healthy. Exercising can make it easier to relax and fall into deep sleep quicker. The main function of sleep is to repair and rejuvenate the body so that it is ready for a new day. Athletes who sleep for at least eight hours should wake up feeling energized and refreshed.

THE SECRETS OF GOOD HEALTH

Scientists now know the keys to keeping a body healthy. Eating right, sleeping well, and exercising regularly are the three ingredients to staying healthy and strong. Consuming a balanced diet of fruits, vegetables, protein, and carbohydrates is vital. Smaller meals tend to keep the body leaner while bigger meals will slow the metabolism down.

A body's metabolism is the speed at which it uses energy it gets through food. A fast metabolism will burn up energy at a faster rate, while slow metabolisms will store excess energy as fat. Generally speaking, fat is harder to burn once it has accumulated. If you're overweight and want to lose weight, you'll need to either cut back on calories (energy in food) or spend more calories (energy) by exercising (or both).

EXERCISE

Exercising is a good way to keep the metabolism moving, and it is also the only way to strengthen the body's muscles. Some of the muscles helped through exercise are skeletal muscles, such as the ones found in the legs and arms. It is easy to see how exercise helps these muscles, because they grow bigger over time. However, there are other muscles that need to be worked out that cannot be seen.

The heart is made of one of the most important types of muscle in the human body—cardiac muscle—and it needs regular exercise to stay in shape. This organ is responsible for bringing oxygen and important *nutrients* to every cell in the body. The heart works with the lungs and skeletal muscles to keep a body in motion.

Fortunately, almost everything the body does will count as some sort of movement. Walking to a friend's house, helping out with yard work, and cleaning up the house are all very easy types of movement. They are not as intense as other exercises, but they are better than sitting on the couch all day or playing on the computer all night.

Sports offer a great way to stay active. Playing sports has physical, mental, and emotional benefits. Sports connect us to others, so they're good ways to make friends and have fun—and stay healthy!

Words to Understand

component: A part of something.
cardiovascular: Having to do with heart and blood vessels.
stamina: The ability to keep exercising for long periods of time without getting too tired to keep going.

Chapter Two
SPORTS
AND MOVEMENT

The human body must be exercised in a number of ways to stay healthy. There are five areas of fitness to pay attention to, known as the five components of physical fitness. They are cardiovascular endurance, muscle endurance, muscle strength, flexibility, and body composition. All sports address at least one **component** of physical fitness, and many sports address most or all of them.

Endurance is a measurement of how much the body can handle before it needs to take a rest. **Cardiovascular** endurance measures how long a human being can run before needing to stop while muscle endurance measures how long a muscle can be exerted before it can't

Doing gymnastics like this requires immense flexibility—but you also need very strong arm muscles to hold a position like this.

Make Connections

A new form of sports was born in the twentieth-century—strength athletics. These are based on the demonstrations of proof that have taken place for many years at circuses and at events from the British Islands known as Highland Games. Strength athletics combines these with elements of powerlifting and weightlifting, along with a range of events involving the lifting of rocks, refrigerators, pulling vehicles (trains, trucks, and planes).

be used anymore. Any sports that involve extended periods of running build endurance. Long-distance running, cross-country skiing, and rowing are three sports that improve cardiovascular and muscle endurance.

Muscle strength, on the other hand, is the measurement of how much a muscle can lift at once. Unlike with endurance training, the muscle does not need to be used very long; it just needs to work a lot at one time. Weightlifting and powerlifting are sports that build muscle strength. Bodybuilders have a lot of muscle strength.

Flexibility—the ability to move and bend—is an important component of physical fitness. Stretching before and after a sports event or game is important because it prepares the muscles for activity, but it also improves the flexibility of the muscles that will get used. Yoga and tai chi are two other ways to improve flexibility, which you'll need for any sport. Gymnastics is an example of a sport that focuses specifically on flexibility, but it also requires muscle strength.

TYPES OF EXERCISE

There are two main categories of exercise: aerobic and anaerobic. Aerobic means "requiring air," while anaerobic means, "without air." In this case, air means oxygen, which is absorbed into the body through

Hitting a baseball or softball—and then sprinting to first base—requires a burst of strength, but you don't get a chance for much aerobic exercise during a baseball game.

the lungs. The cardiovascular system is responsible for carrying oxygen throughout the body, starting with the heart.

Every cell in the body requires oxygen to function. This oxygen is brought to every cell through the cardiovascular system. When the

Aerobic exercises will do wonders to increase endurance, but the most physically fit people use a combination of aerobic and anaerobic exercises. The aerobic ones improve endurance and heart health, while the anaerobic ones are used to strengthen the other muscles in the body. Stronger muscles are less likely to become injured after prolonged use, so the extra effort is never wasted.

human body exerts itself during aerobic exercise, it needs more oxygen than usual to function. Aerobic exercises greatly improve cardiovascular and muscle endurance because they force the heart and skeletal muscles to work harder than normal for a long period of time.

A strong heart and lungs will be able to keep up with the increased oxygen demands of aerobic exercise. The breathing rate speeds up to bring more oxygen into the body while the heart rate also increases. All of this is done to bring oxygen to the cells of the body at a faster pace. Aerobic exercise builds cardiovascular endurance.

Anaerobic exercises do not work out the heart or lungs. They focus on intensity rather than **stamina**, and require huge bursts of energy. Lifting heavy weights and sprinting across a room for a short period of time are two examples of anaerobic exercises. These kinds of workouts build muscle strength more than cardiovascular endurance.

Balanced workouts include both aerobic and anaerobic exercises, because both are needed to address all areas of physical fitness. Most sports have some combination of both kinds of exercise, with some sports having more of one than the other. Different sports may also develop a particular kind of fitness more than another.

Basketball, which requires lots of running back and forth throughout a game, is a great sport for getting lots of aerobic exercise.

Sports & Fitness

BASEBALL AND SOFTBALL

Baseball and softball are primarily anaerobic sports. These sports focus on muscle strength and sprinting. A player who is up at bat will hit the ball with the bat, which requires muscle strength in the arms and shoulders. If she is successful at hitting the ball, she will need to sprint to the first base as fast as she can!

A pitcher in the field needs to have strong arm muscles to throw a fast pitch. The stronger his muscles are, the faster the ball will fly. Faster balls are harder to hit, so a good pitcher needs to train for muscle strength. The other players in the field also need to be great at throwing and catching balls, as this is the only way to prevent the batter from scoring a home run.

When a batter makes a hit, it can go anywhere in the field. If it goes far, players in the outfield will need to sprint very fast to retrieve the ball and toss it to someone who can prevent the batter from scoring a point. Sprinters who are fast enough may even catch the ball before it hits the ground, automatically disqualifying the batter.

There is no prolonged running in the game, so the lungs and heart do not get a good workout. Baseball and softball players should set aside some special time each week to work on aerobic activities, such as jogging or running. All people need aerobic exercise to stay fit and healthy, even great baseball and softball players!

BASKETBALL

Basketball has a healthy amount of both aerobic and anaerobic exercise. Players are constantly jogging down the court to keep up with their teammates and opponents, which is aerobic exercise. Because balls can soar through the air from one end of the court to the other, players will also need to sprint often, and sprinting is a form of anaerobic exercise.

Dribbling, jumping, and dunking are all skills basketball players need, and they all require a lot of muscle strength and some flexibility. Even the strongest athlete wouldn't be able to jump very high without

If you play football regularly, you're getting good anaerobic and aerobic workouts. You're also building strength and flexibility.

Sports & Fitness

practice. A regulation basketball hoop is ten feet high, so an adult basketball player who is six feet in height needs to jump at least four feet above his own head to score a slam dunk!

Lifting weights will also give players the strength they need for long shots. Aiming a ball at a hoop from far away requires a lot of muscle strength; you can't just chuck the ball at the hoop.

Shooting a basketball into the basket requires a certain form or stance. Players need to reach up with the ball in hand and snap their hands and wrists in the right direction. Being off by merely an inch can mean the difference between scoring a point and missing. Flexibility is important here.

Each basketball team has five players on the court, with many other players waiting on the sidelines. Coaches usually put players who are more skilled and in better shape on the court for longer periods because their lungs and heart can handle it. All basketball players must work hard to stay in shape by running and jogging outside of practice. There is added pressure during a game because every player has to stay near her mark—an opponent on the opposite team. That way, she can steal the ball or block a shot if the opponent she is covering has the ball. Being forced to keep up with an opponent pushes basketball players to have quick hands and feet.

Basketball is great exercise, but you can also get hurt playing. If you're going to play basketball, be sure to spend plenty of time stretching before games so you don't injure your knees or legs.

FOOTBALL

Football is one of the most physically intense sports you can play. While most sports have rules against players touching each other, football encourages players to slam into each other to block the other team from making progress in the game.

Football is played on a large rectangular field. Players wear thick padding and helmets to ensure their safety as they ram into each other. Only a few players actually get to touch the ball and throw it down the

Soccer players run constantly during a game, so they need good cardiovascular and muscle endurance. Otherwise, they'll be too tired to keep playing.

field. The other players are there to prevent the other team from stopping the person with the ball—and the only way to stop an opponent who has the football is to knock him down with a tackle. The next play then begins where that tackle occurred, with every single player lined up in a straight line across the field. Every inch of a play counts, so football players throw their bodies on top of the person carrying the ball again and again.

Football players spend a lot of time running down the field after other players, so they get a lot of aerobic exercise in the process. The anaerobic aspect comes in when they are pushing or jumping onto opponents. Football players usually have very thick arm and leg muscles. These muscles make tackling easier. Football players get these muscles from working out outside of the game.

Passing, throwing, and catching a football after it has been thrown long distances is a skill that must be learned to play the sport well. Losing control of a ball at any point is known as a fumble, and it could lead to the other team gaining possession of the ball. Wide receivers need to be able to twist and stretch to catch a ball, as that's their main job on the field, which requires flexibility.

WRESTLING

Wresting is a physically intense sport that is mostly anaerobic. One wrestler tries to pin another to the ground in order to be declared the winner. Competitors are divided into different weight classes to ensure fairness.

There is little cardiovascular exercise done while wrestling. The sport relies almost entirely on muscle strength. Wrestlers spend a lot of time training muscle endurance and strength. Muscle endurance is important because it keeps the wrestler from getting tired during long matches.

SOCCER

Soccer is played on a large field like football is, except a circular ball is kicked around in soccer. Players take turns dribbling the ball down

Lacrosse players use sticks with nets on the end to scoop up the ball and put it through the goal. Lacrosse can be a rough sport so players wear protective gear while playing.

Make Connections: Other Field Sports

Football and soccer are just two of the many field sports. Some lesser-known field sports are lacrosse and field hockey. Both sports are similar to football and soccer in that they require a lot of cardiovascular endurance, but they are different in that these sports use tools to transport the ball across the field. Lacrosse players use a small net to cradle the ball as it moves from player to player. Players can pass the ball using that net, but they may never touch the ball with their hands. Field hockey players use wooden sticks to move the ball, thus making their hockey sticks an extension of themselves.

the field with their feet. Strong leg muscles are an absolute must when playing soccer, as the ball must eventually be kicked into an opposing team's goal to score a point. Fast, hard kicks are harder to block by the opponent's goalkeeper, so players with a fast, hard kick have a clear advantage.

Every soccer player except the goalkeeper is constantly running up and down the field as the ball changes possession. This movement requires a lot of cardiovascular endurance, which is built through aerobic exercise. Leg muscles are built through anaerobic exercises such as heavy lifting at a gym. The feet must also be strong, too, because they will be running fast and kicking the ball a lot. Flexibility is required for quick foot movements.

Dribbling doesn't just function as a way to bring the ball down the field; it is also used to change the ball's direction and speed. Soccer coaches lead players through dribbling exercises to improve their agility, or ability to move quickly. Soccer players must have great foot skills to ensure fast play. Passing the ball to a teammate should feel almost effortless.

Golf is a relaxing hobby for many people, but also a fiercely competitive sport at the professional level.

Sports & Fitness

Make Connections:
The Social and Emotional Benefits of Sports

Researchers in the Netherlands have found that one of the hidden benefits of playing sports is gaining friends and having a higher self-esteem than people who do not play sports. According to the study, people who play sports frequently are less likely to experience anxiety, get into trouble, and be aggressive with others.

Research has also shown that playing sports can improve your mood and reduce stress. People who exercise regularly are less likely to feel depressed as well. All these great mental effects are due to the hormones released during repeated physical activity. One type of hormone, known as endorphins, makes people feel good after exercising. It is a chemical reward for working hard.

Most soccer players do not receive a lot of training in their arms because those muscles are not used often during soccer. However, goalkeepers should have stronger arms than the rest of their team because they need to be able to block a shot from getting into the net. Soccer goalkeepers wear a lot of padding to keep their bodies safe.

GOLF

Golf requires muscle strength and precision. Golfers need to know exactly how hard to hit the ball, which comes with time and experience. Because the ball is so small, it is easily affected by wind and weather. Golfers adjust their shot to account for the changing wind patterns as they play.

With the exception of walking from hole to hole, there is absolutely zero cardiovascular exercise done while playing golf. Unlike other sports, every golf course is a little bit different. The distance to the hole and the traps in between vary from course to course. Golfers must be versatile, or capable of adjusting to new situations, in order to win competitions.

TENNIS

Tennis players are constantly moving on their feet, but they do not move very long distances. Players take turns passing the ball back and forth over a net while trying to score a point by having the ball bounce out of an opponent's court. In order to return a serve, players must dash across the court quickly. This counts as anaerobic exercise.

Players use a heavy racket to hit the ball, which builds the muscle endurance and strength in their arms. They also work out their leg muscles while dashing from one end of the court to the other. Like baseball players, tennis players should spend time outside of the court practicing aerobic exercises. These exercises will help the player's endurance on the court.

Text-Dependent Questions

1. What are the five components of physical fitness, and why are they important?
2. What do aerobic and anaerobic mean?
3. Explain why baseball and softball are considered purely anaerobic sports.
4. How will lifting heavy weights help you become better at throwing a basketball long distances?
5. Why is football considered one of the most physically intense sports?
6. What is agility, and why do soccer players need it?
7. Why do tennis players need muscle endurance?
8. List the sports that require the most cardiovascular endurance.

BOTTOM LINE

Whatever sport you play, you'll probably need some other form of exercise in addition to the sport in order to develop all the elements of fitness you need. Athletes usually run, lift weights, and stretch in addition to practicing for their sport.

But the good thing about sports is that they motivate you to keep exercising. As every athlete knows, practice makes perfect. Being good at a sport takes years of hard work. Even if you're playing a sport just for fun, you'll enjoy seeing your skills improve—and meanwhile, you'll be physically fit!

Words to Understand

interval: A period of time with a definite beginning and a definite end.

succession: One following after another.

Chapter Three

TRAINING FOR SPORTS

No athlete, no matter how good she is today, started out that way. She went through a lot of training first. And no athlete will maintain his skills and fitness level without regular training. In fact, most sports have off seasons when players focus only on training.

During training, athletes aim to perform a combination of aerobic and anaerobic exercises, as well as a mix of exercises that will contribute to the five components of fitness. Overworking yourself during training isn't a good idea, though. Experienced athletes suggest exercising for five days a week, reserving at least one day for complete rest.

Running for long distances or long periods of time requires good cardiovascular endurance. Your legs can't keep doing their job without your heart sending enough oxygen-filled blood to them!

Sports & Fitness

Individual exercises should last at least fifteen to thirty minutes, with different days being used for different exercises. This gives tired muscles time to rest after an intense workout. Performing the same workout each day can strain even the fittest muscles.

ENDURANCE TRAINING

Athletes with a lot of cardiovascular and muscle endurance are able to continue exercising for long periods of time without getting tired. People who play sports need this endurance to continue playing at their best, even during a long and exhausting sport game. They do this with endurance training.

The only way to improve endurance is to build it slowly over time. Following an exercise plan is a great way to stay on track. The endurance built during regular exercise will decrease during periods of inactivity, so athletes must continue to exercise regularly even when they aren't playing sports. Fortunately, there are many options for athletes looking to build endurance.

Running, bicycling, rowing, and swimming are some aerobic exercises that help build cardiovascular endurance. The heart and lungs are forced to work harder than usual during full body exercises because every cell in the body needs more oxygen to function as it is moving more than usual. Through repeated exercise, the heart and lungs will have an easier time delivering that oxygen to the rest of the body.

Endurance exercises will also strengthen the skeletal muscles attached to the bones in your body. The legs, feet, arms, and chest will eventually have an easier time moving and keeping up with the heart and lungs after repeated exercise. Muscular endurance is needed to run, jump, and throw balls during sports.

Unfortunately, there can be a negative side effect to training exercises. During prolonged activity, lactic acid is released into the muscles as a way to give the muscles extra energy to continue functioning. This lactic acid is responsible for the soreness and stiffness many athletes feel after a long workout. The best way to avoid lactic acid buildup is to stretch the muscles after they have been working hard.

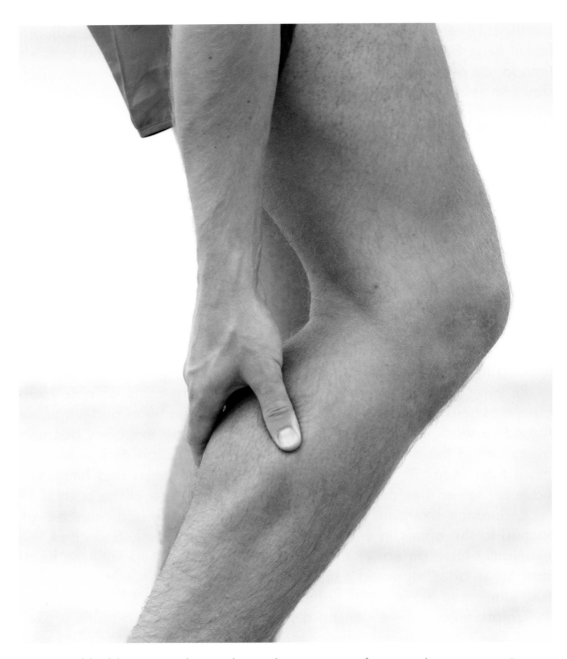

Lactic acid buildup in muscles is what makes you sore after a workout session. As your body becomes more fit, you'll find you're not as sore.

For a workout to be effective, it must last anywhere between fifteen and thirty minutes. Athletes should push themselves, but not too hard, as injuries can cause them to take steps backward in their training. All exercises should begin with warm-ups and end with cool-downs, with at least one day of the week reserved for complete rest.

INTERVAL TRAINING

When athletes train, sometimes they use a technique called *interval* training. Rather than exercising nonstop for fifteen to thirty minutes, athletes who use interval training take regular breaks between sudden bursts of activity. However, they never actually stop moving.

A runner using interval training might run for two minutes, walk for two minutes, and then run for another two minutes before walking again. These intervals have several benefits. Interval training helps the body deal with lactic acid more efficiently because it has a chance to remove the lactic acid during periods of rest. Athletes who use interval training will be able to exercise longer without feeling pain or soreness.

Researchers at the American College of Sports Medicine have discovered that short bursts of activity with equal periods of rest, rather than long stretches of exercise, are also more likely to cause athletes to burn more calories. (A calorie is a measurement of the energy used when a human is exercising, and it plays a role in weight loss.)

Another reason interval training is one of the best ways to exercise is because it forces the body to adapt to changing situations. Because of this, it is the perfect type of training for people who play sports! For example, basketball players do not spend their entire time on the court running and jumping. They may jog from one end of the court to the other most of the time, sprinting only when getting into position to make a shot or block an opponent. Jogging is a low-intensity workout, while sprinting is a high-intensity workout. A basketball player performs both types of workouts on the court. Interval training prepares basketball players—and other athletes—for situations they will encounter every day while playing the sports that they love.

All athletes must be cautious not to overuse their muscles during

Many treadmills have the option of using them for interval training. You can set the machine for periods of fast running on a steep slope, followed by slower running on the level.

The different machines in a gym are ideal for circuit training.

training. Injuries are more likely to happen to athletes who train too much. Fortunately, interval training has been shown to prevent injuries. The high-intensity portions of the exercise plan force the athlete's body to prepare for high-stress situations, while the low-intensity workouts give the athlete's muscles time to rest and recover.

Athletes who are just starting to use interval training should begin with small intervals, such as thirty seconds of full running, followed by thirty seconds of brisk walking. Once athletes become comfortable with the thirty-second intervals, they can consider increasing each interval to one minute. These intervals should never be increased too quickly, as this can increase the likelihood of injury.

CIRCUIT TRAINING

Another effective form of training is circuit training. Unlike interval training, circuit training uses more than one type of exercise. Each exercise is

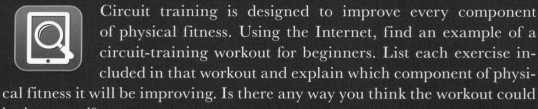
performed in order, forming a cycle, or circuit. Rest is allowed between each individual exercise. When all exercises are completed once, the athlete may take a break before beginning the second set. Athletes just starting out with circuit training should not exceed three circuits.

One of the advantages of circuit training is that it pays attention to every area of physical fitness, not just endurance or strength training. The ideal circuit training routine will have athletes working on their flexibility, muscular endurance, cardiovascular endurance, and muscle strength in *succession*. Like interval training, circuit training requires a certain amount of timing. One example of a circuit plan would include sixty seconds of each exercise, with about fifteen seconds of rest before the next exercise should be done.

While each athlete's individual goals will vary, circuit training can take as little as forty-five minutes per day, with the athlete working out only three to four days a week. A gym membership would be very useful for circuit training, since a typical circuit-training plan requires about ten exercises in each set. These exercises may include sit-ups, pushups, pull-ups, weight training, and running.

Circuit training is particularly useful for athletes who need a well-rounded workout. For example, a soccer player who runs and kicks a

1. According to the author, how many days should an experienced athlete be working out and how many days should be reserved for rest?
2. Why should athletes continue to exercise regularly even when they aren't playing sports?
3. Explain how aerobic exercise improves both cardiovascular and muscular endurance.
4. How does interval training prevent lactic acid buildup in the body?
5. Give an example of a high-intensity workout and a low-intensity one.
6. What is the main difference between circuit training and interval training?
7. How long should an athlete rest between each individual exercise during circuit training?

lot might have strong legs and feet but weak arms because those limbs aren't used as often during soccer. Circuit training will work out every area of the body, leading to greater overall fitness. Circuit training routines ensure that athletes do not neglect one area of the body in favor of another.

WHAT'S RIGHT FOR YOU?

All athletes are different. Fortunately, most exercise plans can be combined or tweaked to fit the individual needs of each athlete depending on their fitness level and future goals. Finding the right exercise plan may take some trial and error. No matter which exercise plan you choose to follow, the most important lesson to remember is that you must stick with it! A strong body takes a long time to build, but it is always worth it in the end.

Words to Understand

fatigue: Extreme tiredness.
effective: Able to do a job well.
chronic: Something that lasts a long time and doesn't go
   away.
inflamed: Sore, red, and swollen.

Chapter Four

SPORTS SAFETY

D ue to the physical nature of sports, playing them comes along with the risk of injury. Knowing the rules of the game, wearing the right safety equipment, and listening to your coach are just some of the ways you can reduce the risk of injury. Unfortunately, sometimes accidents happen. Knowing how to handle an injury will not only help you, but also the people you play with, who are depending on you to do your best for the team.

BEFORE STARTING

Athletes begin getting ready for a day of playing sports long before actually warming up. Eating a large meal before practice is one of the

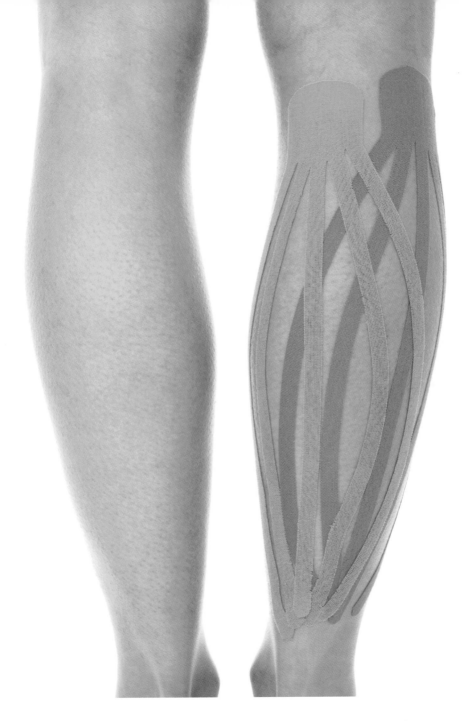

Think of your muscles as big stretchy rubber bands. Stretching them before you exercise means they will be able to do their job better: they'll be able to pull your bones back and forth faster and more powerfully.

Make Connections: The Function of Sweat

One of the body's natural reactions to exercise is to start sweating. Sweat serves two very important purposes. The first purpose is to help the body cool down. Sweat that forms on the body will eventually evaporate into the air, making the body cooler. The second function of sweat is to remove waste from the body. Sweating is an important part of the excretory system, which handles the removal of liquid waste through sweat, exhalation, and urine.

ways athletes ensure they will have enough energy to exercise for hours at a time. Carbohydrates and proteins are an important part of fueling before playing a sport. The carbohydrates provide energy, while the proteins repair and fuel the muscles that will be used.

About 60 percent of the human body is made up of water, and a lot of that water is expelled out of the body through sweat and urine. Active people require more water than inactive people, and the increase in sweat is just one of the reasons athletes need to drink a lot of water. Anyone who does not drink enough water risks becoming dehydrated.

Dehydration is not at all good for the body. Symptoms include dry mouth, dizziness, and *fatigue*. The immune system of a dehydrated person is less *effective* at fighting off infection and disease, making it easier for a dehydrated person to get sick. People who become dehydrated in very hot weather may get overheated because their body has run out of ways to cool itself down.

WARMING UP

Warm-ups are as important as exercising itself. Stretching muscles will strengthen one of the five components of physical fitness: flexibility. Before a muscle is exercised, it is usually tight and stiff. Stretching it will

A lunge, shown here, is a good way to stretch out your thigh and calf muscles, as well as other muscles in your hips and abdomen (your belly).

ensure that it is ready for a long workout, and it will also allow more blood and oxygen to flow to the areas that need it during the exercise.

Warming up also prevents muscles from getting injured during a workout. Without properly warming up, muscles can become strained or even torn! Just a few minutes of warm-up activity can mean the difference between a strong muscle and an injured muscle. Here are four sample warm-up exercises:

- Calf stretches: This stretch will ensure that the muscles in the back of the lower leg are ready for extended movement. One way to stretch each calf is by leaning against a wall, with one leg in front of the other. The front leg should be slightly bent with the back leg stretched out behind. It should be possible to see the toes of the front leg when looking down. The back calf is the one being stretched. Repeat this exercise for each leg.
- Lunges: This stretch affects muscles in the abdomen, hips, and legs. There are many variations of lunges, but the easiest to perform is the forward lunge, done by leaning forward while putting all of the body's weight on the front leg. The front leg should be bent so that the thigh becomes parallel with the floor, while the back leg should nearly be touching the floor. Lunges may be repeated several times.

A football player's helmet, shoulder pads, and cleats are all designed to keep him safe and help him play his sport.

Make Connections: Shoes

 One of the most important pieces of equipment an athlete has is a good pair of shoes. Each type of sport requires a different pair of shoes. Basketball players need sneakers that support fast movement and protect the arches when the athlete jumps. Baseball, football, and soccer players use cleats because the studs on the bottom of the cleats make it easier to run on grass.

- Shoulder stretches: This stretch will keep the shoulders nice and loose during any workout that involves movement of the arms. It is performed by reaching one arm straight out, while pushing it against the chest by bending the other arm. The hips and shoulders should remain aligned throughout the exercise. After a few seconds, switch arms.
- Neck stretches: You may not think you use your neck during sports, but the neck moves a lot during exercise, so it is important to stretch it properly before getting started. Face the head toward the chest and gently push it down using your hands. This will stretch the muscles that support the back of the neck.

EQUIPMENT

Many sports require players to wear safety equipment for their own protection. Football players, for example, must wear helmets, padding, and even mouth guards. Soccer players use padding to protect their legs from harm while kicking the ball around the field. Even wrestlers use padded helmets to prevent injury.

Safety equipment can eventually wear out, which is why it is important to check regularly for any wear and tear. A helmet that is cracked won't protect the head as well as a solid helmet, and padding with

You may not always agree with the referee's calls during a game, but his job is to make sure the game is played safely according to the rules.

holes won't protect the body well at all. If your equipment is broken or faulty, it should be replaced.

Similarly, some sports require extra equipment to actually play the game. Tennis players need tennis rackets, and golf players need golf clubs. Extra pieces of equipment are not toys. Be responsible with the equipment you use; sports equipment should never be swung around haphazardly. Most of this equipment is made out of hard plastic or wood, so accidentally knocking someone on the head with it could cause a serious injury!

Make Connections: Seasonal Sports

Some sports are only played during certain seasons of the year, which is why many students who enjoy sports choose to play two each year: one in the spring and one in the fall. The winter and summer breaks are a good time to take a break from sports and rest. Even professional athletes enjoy an off-season. That doesn't mean, though, that you should stop training during these times!

COOLING DOWN

Athletes should never stop moving immediately after a workout. Muscles need to be slowly eased back into a less active state, and the best way to do this is to perform some exercises that are less stressful on the body before you stop moving altogether. If you have been running, for example, slowing down to a brisk walk is a good way to cool down.

Stretching is also an important part of cool-downs. It serves an entirely different purpose from stretching before a workout. Instead of preparing the muscles for activity, cool-down stretches help the muscles heal after intense activity. They also prevent the muscles from becoming tight.

Muscles that are used for a long time require more oxygen than usual. Lactic acid is released into muscles that aren't receiving enough oxygen to help them keep moving through a workout. Unfortunately, lactic acid can build up in muscles and lead to soreness over the next few days. Stretching prevents this buildup from happening.

LISTEN TO AUTHORITY

Coaches are more than just people who encourage you to practice. They are experts at the game you are learning, and know how to play

Having asthma doesn't mean you can't play sports. You should talk to your doctor first, though, and make sure you always have your inhaler with you at games and whenever you're training or practicing.

Sports & Fitness

it in the safest way possible. Always listen to every rule your coach teaches you, and follow it exactly. Those rules are there to keep you safe while you play the game.

Coaches often begin practice with a lot of warm-ups followed by drills and finally team play. All these steps serve a purpose: they prepare your body for the game you are about to play. Cooling down after practice is also important. Skipping any of these steps could result in bodily injury.

If at any point you have a question, you should ask your coach, especially if it is health related! Many coaches are trained in the use of first aid, and they will have first-aid kits on hand. They will know what to do if you are injured or sick, and they should always put your health above winning a game. Never be afraid to speak up if you feel you just can't play anymore.

A referee is another authority you have to listen to. Referees serve two important functions. The most obvious purpose they have is scoring the game and making sure everyone is following the rules. The second, even more important function is to make sure the play environment is safe. If someone is injured on the field, the referee will immediately call a time-out to help that person. All players must stop playing immediately and listen to any directions they are given.

LISTEN TO YOUR BODY

Before enrolling in a sport, go to a doctor for a routine examination. Tell her which sport you would like to play, and she will be able to tell you if you are healthy enough to play it. Some athletes have certain medical conditions that can make playing sports more difficult, such as asthma. Fortunately, asthma is treatable with the use of an inhaler. Most people who have asthma may find their condition actually improves with regular exercise.

Even the fittest body needs attention. Always bring a lot of water to practice with you, and drink as much of it as you can before, during, and after practice. Never play sports on an empty stomach, as this could cause you to become tired very fast—but don't try to exercise

A sports drink can be good if you're going to be exercising in hot weather or for a long time, since it will help you replace some of the chemicals you lose when you sweat. Other times, though, you'd do better sticking with water, since sports drinks contain almost as much sugar and calories as soda.

after a heavy meal either! Bring a healthy snack with you to practice if you will be playing for a while.

Never push yourself beyond your comfort zone. If you aren't feeling well, tell your coach and take a rest. Playing sports while you're sick will only make your sickness worse. Athletes who are sick or getting over an illness should take a break from playing sports in order to rest and get better. You also need to stay away from your teammates when you are sick, so they don't catch whatever you have!

INJURIES

Even athletes who are very careful can sometimes get injured while playing the game they love. A basketball player could twist her ankle

Make Connections: Sports Drinks

Sports drinks get their name from the fact that they help keep athletes energized and hydrated during long periods of activity. These drinks contain fluid, carbohydrates, and sodium (salt). The carbohydrates will boost an athlete's energy, while the sodium will replenish the sodium lost through sweat during a prolonged workout. Athletes should only use sports drinks if they are working out for more than a few hours, though, as sports drinks can lead to weight gain if consumed by people who do not exercise regularly. They are technically classified as soft drinks, and they contain a lot of sugar and calories.

after landing from a jump shot, or a soccer player could trip and fall while kicking the ball into the goal. Not all injuries are serious, but every injury should be taken care of when it happens. Even a tiny scrape should be washed and covered before an athlete returns to play.

Accidents happen, and the best way to deal with them is to know what to do. If you are ever hurt on the field, let someone know immediately. The worst thing you can do when you have an injury is try to keep playing. Putting weight or stress on a body part that is already injured runs the risk of making the injury worse. A strained muscle could easily turn into a torn muscle, which will take a lot more time and care to heal than the original injury.

Acute injuries are ones that occur because of some sort of trauma while playing sports, but there is another type of injury that all athletes are at risk of developing: *chronic* injuries. Believe it or not, you can exercise too much! Chronic injures occur when the body is used more than it should be, which is why it is important to get enough rest outside of practice.

Overuse injuries include stress fractures, tendinitis, and epiphysitis.

Bones that experience a lot of stress will weaken and crack over time, causing stress fractures. Jumping a lot, such as a basketball player does when shooting, could cause stress fractures in the feet. Tendinitis occurs when a tendon, which is attached to the muscle, is overstretched through repeated use. It becomes **inflamed** and painful as a result. Epiphysitis is most common in children with growing bodies who are going through a growth spurt. As the body grows, growth plates move and shift to make room for the other bones and muscles that are growing as well. Overuse of the areas that are shifting could cause a number of growth plate issues, which may also cause inflamed tendons.

The best way to fix chronic injuries is to take a break from playing sports. A cold ice pack can be used to reduce swelling until you see a doctor. Ask your doctor how the injury should be treated, and follow those directions exactly. Do not start playing again until you are given approval from the doctor. People with chronic injuries should consider using a less intense workout plan when they finally return to playing sports.

BALANCE

Students who play sports can have a very busy schedule. Going to school, practicing for a sport, and attending competitions take up a

Text-Dependent Questions

1. What are the effects of dehydration and how can they be prevented?
2. Explain why it is important to stretch before and after playing sports.
3. According to the author, what equipment is needed to play football? What about soccer?
4. What are the two functions of a referee?
5. Why shouldn't you play sports when you are sick?
6. What are the two categories of sports injuries and how are they different?

good portion of the week. Athletes in school need to find the time to do their homework, exercise, and see friends too.

Being a dedicated athlete can feel overwhelming at first, which is why it is important to find a balance between everything you do. Priorities must be chosen, with schoolwork and getting enough rest coming first. School administrators agree that sports should come second to schoolwork, which is why many schools won't even allow students who fall below a certain grade-point average to stay on a sports team.

Making a weekly schedule is an easy way to keep track of how your time is spent. Dedicating an hour or two to homework each day gives you enough time to practice your sport, see friends, and still exercise on a regular basis. By planning your schedule ahead of time, you are less likely to bite off more than you can chew.

Playing sports has many benefits. It improves mental and emotional well-being. It's a great way to make friends. People who play sports are less likely to become ill, and more likely to recover faster following an illness. Most important of all, it provides a fun way to exercise that doesn't feel boring at all!

FIND OUT MORE

In Books

Bounds, Laura, Kirsten Brekken Shea, Dottiedee Agnor, and Gayden Darnell. *Health & Fitness: A Guide to a Healthy Lifestyle*. Dubuque, Iowa: Kendall Hunt, 2012.

Frederick, Shane. *Stamina Training for Teen Athletes: Exercises to Take Your Game to the Next Level*. North Mankato, Minn.: Capstone, 2012.

Greenfield, Ben. *Beyond Training: Mastering Endurance, Health, and Life*. Las Vegas, Nev.: Victory Belt Publishing, 2014.

Lancaster, Scott B., and Radu Teodorescu. *Athletic Fitness for Kids*. Champaign, Ill.: Human Kinetics, 2008.

Maffetone, Philip, and Mark Allen. *The Big Book of Endurance Training and Racing*. New York: Skyhorse, 2010.

Online

5 Key Components to Physical Fitness
www.abetterbodytraining.com/key_components_to_physical_fitness.html

Endurance Training for Sports
sportsmedicine.about.com/od/anatomyandphysiology/a/Endurance.htm

The Benefits of Physical Activity
www.hsph.harvard.edu/nutritionsource/staying-active-full-story

What's the Best Exercise Plan for Me?
www.helpguide.org/harvard/exercise-plan.htm

Fitness Training: Elements of a Well-Rounded Routine
www.mayoclinic.org/fitness-training/art-20044792

SERIES GLOSSARY OF KEY TERMS

abs: Short for abdominals. The muscles in the middle of your body, located over your stomach and intestines.

aerobic: A process by which energy is steadily released using oxygen. Aerobic exercise focuses on breathing and exercising for a long time.

anaerobic: When lots of energy is quickly released, without using oxygen. You can't do anaerobic exercises for a very long time.

balance: Your ability to stay steady and upright.

basal metabolic rate: How many calories your body burns naturally just by breathing and carrying out other body processes.

bodybuilding: Exercising specifically to get bigger, stronger muscles.

calories: The units of energy that your body uses. You get calories from food and you use them up when you exercise.

carbohydrates: The foods that your body gets most of its energy from. Common foods high in carbohydrates include sugars and grains.

cardiovascular system: Your heart and blood vessels.

circuit training: Rapidly switching from one exercise to another in a cycle. Circuit training helps build endurance in many different muscle groups.

circulatory system: The system of blood vessels in your body, which brings oxygen and nutrients to your cells and carries waste products away.

cool down: A gentle exercise that helps your body start to relax after a workout.

core: The muscles of your torso, including your abs and back muscles.

cross training: When an athlete trains for a sport she normally doesn't play, to exercise any muscle groups she might be weak in.

dehydration: When you don't have enough water in your body. When you exercise, you lose water by sweating, and it's important to replace it.

deltoids: The thick muscles covering your shoulder joint.

energy: The power your body needs to do things like move around and keep you alive.

endurance: The ability to keep going for a long time.

flexibility: How far you can bend, or how far your muscles can stretch.

glutes: Short for gluteals, the muscles in your buttocks.

hydration: Taking in more water to keep from getting dehydrated.

isometric: An exercise that you do without moving, by holding one position.

isotonic: An exercise you do by moving your muscles.

lactic acid: A chemical that builds up in your muscles after you exercise. It causes a burning feeling during anaerobic exercises.

lats: Short for latissimus dorsi, the large muscles along your back.

metabolism: How fast you digest food and burn energy.

muscle: The parts of your body that contract and expand to allow you to move.

nervous system: Made up of your brain, spinal cord, and nerves, which carry messages between your brain, spinal cord, and the rest of your body.

nutrition: The chemical parts of the food you eat that your body needs to survive and use energy.

obliques: The muscles to either side of your stomach, under your ribcage.

pecs: Short for pectorals, the muscles on your chest.

quads: Short for quadriceps, the large muscle on the front of your upper leg and thigh.

reps: How many times you repeat an anaerobic exercise in a row.

strength: The power of your muscles.

stretching: Pulling on your muscles to make them longer. Stretching before you exercise can keep you flexible and prevent injuries.

warm up: A light exercise you do before a workout to get your body ready for harder exercise.

weight training: Exercises that involve lifting heavy weights to increase your strength and endurance.

INDEX

ABOUT THE AUTHOR AND THE CONSULTANT

Celicia Scott lives in upstate New York. She worked in teaching before starting a second career as a writer.

Diane H. Hart, Nationally Certified Fitness Professional and Health Specialist, has designed and implemented fitness and wellness programs for more than twenty years. She is a master member of the International Association of Fitness Professionals, and a health specialist for Blue Shield of Northeastern New York, HealthNow, and Palladian Health. In 2010, Diane was elected president of the National Association for Health and Fitness (NAHF), a nonprofit organization that exists to improve the quality of life for individuals in the United States through the promotion of physical fitness, sports, and healthy lifestyles. NAHF accomplishes this work by fostering and supporting state governors and state councils and coalitions that promote and encourage regular physical activity. NAHF is also the national sponsor of Employee Health and Fitness Month, the largest global workplace health and fitness event each May. American College of Sports Medicine (ACSM) has been a strategic partner with NAHF since 2009.

PICTURE CREDITS